THE BLACK & LATINX POETRY PROJECT

By **ALEGRIA** PUBLISHING

davina@alegriamagazine.com

Ordering Information:
Quantity sales. Special discounts are available on quantity
purchases by corporations, associations, and others. For
details, contact the publisher at
davina@alegriamagazine.com

Orders by U.S. trade bookstores and wholesalers. Please
contact Big Distribution:
www.ingramspark.com

Printed in the United States of America.

Library of Congress Control Number: 2020917483

ISBN: 978-1-7347252-4-7
Artwork by: Sirenas Creative
Editing: Camari Carter

The Black & LatinX Poetry Project

By **ALEGRIA** PUBLISHING

PUBLISHER'S NOTE

Throughout the process of bringing The Black & LatinX Poetry Project to life, my heart has been filled with indescribable joy.

The idea for this magical creative endeavor came to me as I was preparing to publish If Love Had a Name, my very own poetry collection.

As you may know, writing a book can often be a solitary journey. I was ready for a collective project. On this lonely road, driven by individualistic creativity, nothing is more welcome than the spirit of community. As a poet myself, I find inspiration by soaking in the words of fellow poets. While they keep this beautiful art form alive, through artistic collaborations and new digital possibilities, they also enlighten us with their raw and soulful work.

To this day, the publishing industry continues to underrepresent diverse writers and, as a result, deny readers the power and beauty of necessary voices. It is my hope that through an inclusive collection like this, we can amplify relevant cultural narratives and shine a light on the rich humanity contained within our stories.

There are those that would have us believe Black & LatinX poets are extinct or on their way to becoming irrelevant. Nothing is further from the truth. We are very much alive and we are everywhere.

Across the globe, our lives are the very definition of magical realism. We inherited poetry —carried from our ancestors'tongues into the DNA of every generation to follow. It was this longing, this passionate commitment to find new Black & LatinX poets and storytellers, that moved me to create this sacred space.

First, my company,

ALEGRIA Media and Publishing, ran a poetry contest. We opened it to anyone with a desire to talk about immigration, social justice, love and feminism today.

I never imagined such an incredible response. Hundreds of poems were received and I personally read each and every one, literally crying tears of joy.

I had found my tribe. I was not alone.

Thank you for showing up. Thank you for being so vulnerable – for having the courage to share your heart with all of us.

I hope you enjoy The Black & Latinx Poetry Project. Born out of a love for poetry and poets, it brings together more than 20 emerging poets.

The Black & LatinX Poetry Project unites a new generation of Black and Brown poets in one book. It is my dream for this launch to skip like a stone across the water's surface, creating an ever-widening ripple effect, reflecting the magnitude of our human potential. May it be the beginning of creative collaborations that carry a lasting impact.

By purchasing this book, you are supporting Black & LatinX artists and storytellers.

Please check @ alegriamagazine for new and upcoming LatinX books & magazines.

Much ALEGRÍA & Poesía Always,

Davina Ferreira

davina@alegriamagazine.com
www.davinaferreira.com
IG @ davifalegria

BLACK JOY

The root of my most precious peace
is watching the clouds dance

They're made up of the tears
of their ancestors

Just like me, just like us

Their colors and textures, varied
and sensual, sun-laced

Just like me, just like us

They remind me of what can be beautiful
about belonging nowhere

When I'm weary
and the earth
is the only thing to hold me

I look up and sing to them
"To be free, to be free, to be free"

They answer in the wind
with their dance
They rain down their peace into me

But soft like a kiss, an invitation

And for a moment, I stop thinking
about how long, such a short life can feel

And I let joy rise up in me

I let my hope hang between the space
in my chest normally reserved for grief

I let my toes dance with the clouds

I sing Louis Armstrong's What A Wonderful World

And I let myself imagine the world in exactly that way

They say that we are our ancestors' wildest dreams

And in that moment, I believe that.

By Jade

WHAT IS LOVE?

By: LexUni

They say love is
Something like
The finest
Drug
Love
Gives your
Heart that tug
And
Speaking about hearts
I wear mine on
My chest
Like a glove
My armor is
Love
That's how
That's why
I spread peace
Without the
Love and peace
The world
Leads
To mass destruction
As you can see
Justice be
To all who
Still don't feel free
It is time my fellow
Beings
To set your
Own soul free
Can't leave it up
To the
Men who
Put us in cages
Provoke
Our inner rage
And
Forgive me or don't
But the government
Seems like a decoy

To corrupt your
Soul
For the gain of
Control
It's time for us
To stand up and say
NO!!
Spiritual freedom
Is what we demand
Together is how we stand
Love peace and joy
Fills our hearts
We spread high
frequency
Maneuvering through
This time
Painting the world
Like art
In touch with the divine
It's time
Don't you see?
To truly set your
Soul free
Be one with the wind
One with the trees
One as a unit
The Human race
Not divided
By skin
Only energy
Is what
We see
The time awaits
Us
And
I know this
Because I've been shown
That precious sight
You've been there
once or twice

But
This reality
Make you
Think twice
Whenever you come
Near your spirit
So stay clear
And keep aware
Our time is here
Stay woke y'all
Peace

Awaken the masses
Spread love
Spread peace
Rebuke ALL
Inequity
For we are not equal
We don't fight to be
Equal
We fight to
Be free
From the
Physical world
Imprisonment
We fight to be
Introduced to our spirit
So we can really feel it
Light it up
Our insides
Our within
So we can spread
World peace
Lead each other
To real
Gems
Earth
This universe
Is full
Of them
The road is near
The grand rising

Of our souls
Is here
I love anyone
Who feels this
I love you even more
If you don't
I love the universe
x1000000
For providing the
Wisdom
And guidance
Let's set
Ourselves
Free
And
See
How the
world turns
Automatic
Shift
Of energy
Instant gratification
For the
Divine light
Instant
Healing
To the masses
We
All yearn
For compassion
So how
About we give it
To ourselves first
See how that works
In reverse
Stay woke y'all
Peace.

AFRORIKEN

By: Adassa

Afroriken pride in our enslaved skin
Warrior spirit breaking the chains within
The beat of the drum where rhythm resides
Looking out cuevas through windowed eyes
Arawak and African strength of armored wisdom
Tattered paved roads in a jeweled jungle our
kingdom
Intertwined roots uniting us as one
For colorism and racism making minds undone
Striking down on bamboo with a dull machete
This oppression
This obsession
To try and break free
Boriken land singing among the coqui strong
and loud
Our ancestors' spirits guidance to stand united
and proud.

IMAGINE

By: : Kerry B

I heard Jimi said it best, "When the power of love overcomes

the love of power; the world will know peace."

Can you imagine a world without walls or boundaries, where neighbors can shake hands?

Think of a world where you left Tennessee to go to Toronto to ask for some maple syrup for your fresh pancakes.

Can you imagine a world that forgot about war? The definition of a foe would disappear and replaced with that of a friend.

A society that wouldn't know what a gun was unless they saw it on the History channel.

No more violence, just natural causes As souls gently escape in the breeze while families mourn with more peace and tranquility.

Can you imagine a world without greed? Every dollar would be treated as a tumbleweed amongst the plains of civilization.

Food and fellowship would be more valuable as the ones with the most love become the richest. No tricks for the trade, everybody will get paid

All with a simple handshake.

Imagine.

HOME SISTERS

Do you think if we cry enough tears
to fill up every room we find ourselves in,
we will float up one day
and break through the ceilings they have placed on
us?
Or have our hearts become too heavy we sink to the
bottom?
Keep crying. That's okay.
But let's also swim against the current. Break the
door down.
Hold onto me as I hold onto you.
Our tears, a river rushing past us. Let this house be
washed away.
Because what is there left to dry and save and
rebuild
when the foundation was made of scraps to begin
with?
We have a whole new house to build. One without
doors, walls, nor ceilings. No one holds the golden
keys.
All are welcome here. We are finally home.

By: Janette Valenzo

LOVE POEMS

By: Janette Valenzo

I want to write so many love poems for you,
read them out loud for you,
in front of strangers for you,
surrounded by family and friends for you,
have line after line for you
papers scattered all over our bodies for
you, no ending in sight for you
no ending for you,
I want to write love poems
but only if you are here with me
to read them with me –
I'll even read them for you with me
but you have to be here with me
I'm tired of trying to write love poems
when we keep having to defend our love first
can I please spare a few words to write a
love poem for you with me?
let me write you a love poem, let me write a
poem,
let me write you, love.

ALEGRIA PUBLISHING

FOR MY TRANS SISTERS TOO

To all the men who have stolen from me

I hope my words

hit you

like a wall.

I pray the shame
You
Feel
Looking
Into
The
Mirror

Breaks

You

The

Same way

You hoped

To break

Me

When you

held
my
nose like

a dog

rubbing it into your version

of right and wrong.

Never

Before

Enjoying

Your

Privilege

So much.

Your
Entitlement
Is
Not
an
Acquittal.

and
Your
One-sided
Sense
Of

By: Jade

Virtue
And
Twisted
Justice

is child-like.

actually

Your inability to evolve is

Laughable.

But

I suppose.

That is the nature of

Predators.

Thing

is

Women like me

are tired of the

same old

rules

of the
jungle.

Fight or flight?

We are

exhausted

by

the science

of our

so-called

limitations.

We watched

our

mothers'

fight

take

the light

from

their

eyes

and

their

flight

take

them so
far

from

themselves

that

their

daughters

spend

their own

lifetimes

retracing

steps

Do you hear me?

You have

stolen

lifetimes.

This kind

of violation

echoes

into

the

way

that

we

carry

ourselves

but no more.

It

is

time

that

you

get

to
experience

the dog eat dog

nature

of your very

own

hunting ground

spoils

of your

you

pillaging

call

We

us

were

sheep

sharpening our swords.

and treat

us like

bitches

but where

there

are sheep
there's a herd

and bitches

bite back

while

you

were

enjoying

the

LOVE IS A WEAPON

Love is a weapon for all that is unjust,
Love is a tool to fix the brokenness inside,
Love is the key to unlock the healing pathway in this world,
Love transcends beyond this physical world,
The love within grows deeper and stronger as we learn to
embrace all we were created to be, without attachments, without
prejudice.
Knowing we are divinity in the physical, knowing we are love.

By: Jessica Guzman

CONTIGENT LOVE

By: Mikayla Amina Brown

I am tired of contingent love
The type of love where
they want my looks
but not my heart

To them I am:
An idea
A notion
An aesthetic

To them my sole purpose is to
dangle from their arm
like some trendy accessory
Seen but never heard

They want my looks
but not my heart
For my heart is
'too heavy', they say as if
it was purely sacrilegious

But what they fail to realize
is ever since I was a child
I alone have carried
the weight of my mother
the sins of my father
the burdens of my sister
the pain of my ancestors

And while you were too busy
throwing a pity party
for my heart

of which you wrote off as
'baggage'
as a means of excusing
what was just your
inability
to fully love every inch of
me

I was reminded that
I am not what I carry

My heart is not comprised of
the weight of my mother
the sins of my father
the burdens of my sister
the pain of my ancestors

My heart is made of
a love that is bound by
strength
A pureness that is
unwavering
An essence of compassion
A sereneness capable of
ending wars

I am tired of contingent
love
For I am more than my looks
I am love

And I am worthy.

LOVE EXPLORATION

I long to explore our connection
Wanting to get lost in every direction
Just to linger at each intersection
Touching the curves of your soul with a thorough
inspection
Draping my heart over you for protection
So tightly bonded I see you in my reflection
Just to go deeper – injection
Growing love despite our flaws – perfection.

By: Iverson Matthew Jackson

I KNOW...

I know I'm Black, you remind me everyday
You're so persistent in hating my existence
I basically have no choice but to join the resistance
"Look at those 'thugs'," you say
If I'm jogging down the street, going out to eat
or walking home with some Skittles and tea
I get the same police harassment from NYC to LA
Pulling me over if I drive an old Honda or new Rover
One mistake and like that you could decide my life is over

I know I'm Black, you remind me everyday
Confederate flags for "Southern Pride" flown high
To me it symbolizes freedom they tried to deny
"But it's just our heritage", you say
A history of hate, a history of failed Confederate States
That's on display when Neo-Nazis and White Supremacists
congregate
And if I protest peacefully, they tell me, "No, not that way"
"Don't take a knee on TV, or complain about police
brutality,
or point out 400 years of oppression because it annoys me."

I know I'm Black, you remind me everyday
Whether I'm a judge or a janitor I get treated the same way
Education doesn't save you from the discriminatory play
Neither does being wealthy cause money won't buy you sway
In a tailored suit or jeans, our skin gives it right away
Their bigotry and bias only sees it one way:
"If you're Black, you're a criminal and deserve to get put
away."
As if all Blacks have a death wish and it might be our
lucky day
for a new GoFundMe site and a reason for us to pray.

I know... I'm Black. You remind me everyday.

By: Iverson Matthew Jackson

ALEORIA PUBLISHING

OUR WORDS HAVE POWER

Our words have POWER, so I pick up this pen, lace up my
shoes and march to combat your sin.
Fire in my belly, shaking off depression, praying God
forgives me but I wanna teach you a lesson.
Love has taught me to come in peace, though we have been
chained, hogtied, our blood in the streets.
We have to explain why Black Lives Matter as we scream
it loudly until backboards are shattered, until laws are
rewritten, until street signs are named after us, change is
coming, it must, it must, it must.
Justice must be served, silence will never unlock the
chains of oppression, we won't stop until the world has
learned our lesson.

By: Teresa Meade-Mcfarley

MY AMERICA, THE ENTIRE CONTINENT

By: Ramon Jimenez

America,
it smells like an orange blend of hate
that spews insults behind twitter accounts
only to shed Karen tears when confronted.

It looks like 1984,
where big brother tells you one thing
but he really means the opposite.
Things like, "we love families"
translates into, "lock up families"
by separating mothers from children.

America,
It hates its southern neighbors.
Meddles in their affairs.
Contributes to the misery.
But loves dry pieces of avocado toast
on the shores of Puerto Vallarta
taking more shots of tequila
than my Tio Sergio at a quinceañera.

America,
old fashioned and obsolete
like a VHS player stuck on rewind,
a fat floppy disk on the shelf,
a dusty set of typewriter keys,
or a segregated bus from the 1950's.
That's their America.

My America is young and ancient,
never forgetting its past,
immigrant and working class.
Made from all corners of the globe.

Free to speak in the language of its choice,
without the fear of having its mouth washed
out with soap.

My America,
more than the USA
it's the entire continent.
From the frosty extremes of Alaska
to thick and lush Amazonian jungle.
My America is everything.

And while their America,
awkwardly moves its hips,
uselessly attempting to find a rhythm,
that does not exist.
Our America slides to the beat of freedom,
laughing at the embracement of their America
marching until walls are broken
and all cages are swung wide open.

En el mundo que deseo

Nadie se asusta cuando dice negro
sigue siendo de cariño
y no de ese silencio que a veces pasa
A mi madre no le dicen mejora la raza cuando ve a mi
padre
y su papá sigue ahí y nos conocemos
Mi hablar español siendo negra no será de sorpresas
ni de comentarios sarcásticos
de lo bien que habla el español
No tengo que explicar de dónde soy
y a veces cuando estoy en algún sitio
me hablaran español sin pensarlo dos veces
A mi ex novio
no le preguntan si él es hijo de mi madre
porque él parece más "latino"
También me parezco a mi madre
y no solo a mi padre porque soy negra como el
En este mundo que deseo
nadie duda que mi madre
es mi madre
no tenemos que pelear
en la tienda para comprobarlo
Soy libre siendo Boricua y Haitiana
sin tener que dar explicaciones
de como es que soy
Latina y Negra
En esta vida que deseo
no hay separaciones,
nadie maltrate al otro por cómo se ve
somos de verdad ser humanos y no opresión histórica y
continua que deseamos borrar,
verdaderamente importamos
Y celebramos cada cual en su ser
En el mundo que deseo
No tengo que responderle a alguien en español
que me estaba criticando por ser quien soy
Y me responden en español en vez de inglés masticao
En este tiempo nos enamoramos de quien nos da la gana
sin prejuicios
ni pretextos
ni lamentos

By: Lysz Flo

ni explicaciones
No asumen que trabajo en el sitio donde estoy comprando
En el mundo que deseo
soy ser humano y eso es suficiente
Grief
Moves in and rearranges the furniture
Takes control of the remote
Holding your hand all the while
Even on the sunniest of days
Breaking the most gentle of your favorite china
It holds on to your ability to spread
your wings, clinging to your psyche
No poem suffices
No space in between the cracks
It climbs on your back
dragging you/knuckles to ground
Isn't it a strange rainbow
The dark delineated designs in a kaleidoscope
where the deepest love
is now
fractured/ hollowed out & distorted
I look at the sky in those confines,
Seeing colors and reliving shapes
grateful
for the grief I carry
There was love
to be mourned here
Joy to be had
Depression to Overcome
A hero's tale to be told
To see that I have sunsets
with my name engraved in them
I find gratitude
in the intricacies of this weighted grief
mourning so many
versions and visions of me
We all have grief in common
but what about this love
This love
We all have, to give.

BACK TO BLACK

Unarmed Black Man Shot and Killed
This headline is repeatedly revealed
We see it over and over again
We see videos of indisputable proof and murderous sin
And justice still stumbles and fades into the blue.

And... just like that,
We go back to black
Where the odds are stacked
like acres of white picket fences
and being submissive, is dismissible

Where my country warns me
about my hair, my clothes and personality
because at any time
I might be accused of a crime
And if I resist, I could end up dead.

My melanin is not a tattoo or an excuse for abuse
My melanin should not be the mark of social injustice
Furthermore,
violent ends should not be a part of my dark existence

No more cages of poverty
No more racial intimidation
No more segregation
No more men made martyrs met by made-men murderers

Would you be ok with that?
Would you be ok if you woke up... black?

By: ReeNoun

WHITE NOISE

By: Jamilah Muhammad

White noise,
that's all it takes to hurt and harm black girls and boys.
We live in a time where People of Color are stressing,
down on our knees, asking God for a blessing to get us out of
this mess that feels non-stop,
filled with oppression, depression, regression, but has
anyone stopped and thought that the key to progression is not
forgiving or forgetting but standing tall, fighting for your
rights without regretting.

Your actions (only the ones with good intentions though)
will get you through these rough times, but that's that shit
only a Woke Negro would know. Back in the day, they would hose
us to the ground.
That's okay though, because now, they found it more practical to
just gun us down.

If they gunned me down today, which picture would they show?
A demonstration of my accolades or the one with the jail cell
glow?
If I throw away my shot, does that give them the right to shoot at
me, even if I merely just wanted to sell a damn CD?
What if I was outside, enjoying a birthday celebration;
then do they have the right to shoot the shot heard around the
nation?

White noise; that's all I end up hearing.
Because they shot me first, asked questions second when
skepticism began appearing brothers and sisters, please stay
close to your roots.
They're ultimately all you have, don't let them take that from
you, too.

POEM #1

By: Olivia Lapeyrolerie

As a Black Woman, I deserve an Oscar

For all the times I've been hurt but didn't let it show

For all the times I've been the only Black person in the room

For all the times I've been asked to speak on behalf of all Black people

For all the times I've been interrupted

For all the times I've been told I was overreacting

For all the times I've been objectified

For all the times I've been humiliated

For all the times I've had to watch my loved ones be humiliated

For all the thousand cuts little and big I can't recall

I was raised to hold my head up high, just like my ancestors did on the plantation and in the Jim Crow South

But, I can no longer be silent
A river of rage is flowing through me and the dam can no longer hold.

POEM #5

When I was a seedling, I never felt like I
belonged.
No matter how hard I tried,
I could never wiggle into your
Abercrombie jeans.
No matter how hot the comb,
My hair would always rise.

I thought if I tried hard enough,
You wouldn't notice I was a round whole in
your square ass world.
If I just tried harder,
I could shrink into the box of your
expectations.

But as my roots start to grow,
I finally see that my soul was never meant
to fit into your cage.
I was meant to break it.

By: Olivia Lapeyrolerie

MUTED

The walls, the air, the inmates all were mute as eleven strangers walked through.
In soft focus we walked with such great haste, for we were scared to let them see our face. The officer told us to look away.
Because the inmates might begin to sway in a way that might shake us to the core; It was a sight we hadn't seen before.
As I walked through the valley of the shadow of death, I felt the dread and the fear in every breath.
The men put up a front when we walked by, shouting "buss down thotiana!" as opposed to their daily cry.
The men in there were hurting, I could see.
Some we spoke to said they missed their family.
What shocked me the most was what I couldn't see; Hearing them talk about how they wished to cease to be; How no life at all was better than a life in that place.
With the mute walls and the still air and not a single smiling face.
A claustrophobic's worst nightmare is where they lived; The bed, the sink, the toilet together so nothing was hidden. Wake up at 4, eat, sleep, fight, repeat –
seemed to be the inmates' daily feat.
A life filled with constant, which is what some crave.
Because on the outside, you might not be a slave.
But you might not eat and have nowhere to sleep, which makes those cells and sandwiches seem like a benefit to reap.
New Slaves were all that I saw;
Melanated men up and down the hall.
I thought that slavery had ceased to exist, "except as a punishment for crime whereof the party shall have been duly convict." But the Black man was heavily represented at the county jail, mostly as a result of this country's fail.
From juveniles to seniors, they were checked across the board; Waiting for the nurse, getting the only healthcare they can afford. Although they've made mistakes, they need our assistance, which can definitely be done with the right persistence.
Some of these men need advocates to fight for their rights.
Because no matter how loud they shout, their sounds can only reach such heights Until again and again they become Mute.

By: Jamilah Muhammad

CINNAMON PRETZEL

By: Wendy Garcia

Slide down her curls,
Hold on to her wide hips,
Get lost in the abyss of her eyes,
Devour her delicious lips.
She pins you down,
Hold on tight,
Cinnamon pretzel,
Make love all night.

PRETEND

By: Wendy Garcia

Stepping out for a cigarette,
My brown fingers shaking,
Smoke blowing through my curls,
Getting good at faking.
My lips are parched with thirst,
Possibly broken from all the lies,
Smiled a bit too much today,
Cannot tell the lows from highs.
It's time to go back again,
The Man collects tears and sweat,
Sells them for a good price,
As long as you're not a threat.
Keep nodding with approval,
Stay smiling my friend,
Another died in the street again,
I just cannot pretend.

DEFINE

Don't be defined
Let your inner beauty blow their mind
Ignore society's rules and limitations
of their definition of beauty and
imitations
Embrace all that is you and all that you
are
Have a good heart
Be strong
And let your confidence take you far.

By: Adassa

CLAIMING THE SUN

By: Armani Roggers

Hoping I'm open with focus
For this my solo stride a magnum opus
How I've flown with this lotus poetry in motion
Phantom menace fish on the upcoming
Let me show you real gumption
What you know bout ducking mfs who be on dumb shit
Seen niggas switch for a buck quick
Heaven knows how this life shit goes
Either running or bracing for the blows
Face the pressure in prose
Every second I'm golden
Get it from the dirt with the chosen
Kinfolk know I'm a wild child with that wild style
Foul mouth dragon from the proud south
Show you how I get it
Denim fitted
Lenses tinted
What's the business bro
Been lit ten fins ago
This that real spirit flow
My negro spiritual
No rush
For the cold ones when the sun up
Make or break to get the funds up
What you want with us?
We Claim the sun bruh
Run up get done up
You don't want war with us
It's in our blood
We all warriors
And we don't come out to play that
So, stay back or the ground I stand
Will be where your face at.

ALEGRIA PUBLISHING

ODE TO MI GENTE

My parents came to North Carolina, it's the late 80s,
Talk to them in English, said the school system to the
few Mexican ladies.
Did they come to the tobacco field only to lack unity?
It's division they want, stop the hate, and let's build
community.
Walking to school in early winter mornings, hand-
made flour tortilla,
My mother, la Reyna de la cocina.
Mi casa, a refugio for all, my parents didn't say no,
Families came and went, what do you need? My mom can
sew.
Making a living with her hands, mi mama, she loved
everyone,
Chorizo and eggs in the morning,
Multiple families eating together, you better hurry
up and run.
Children playing, adults talking, it's unity and love.

Mi Gente, this is where we were shown to love each
other,
To lend a helping hand to that sister and brother.
Unite as one, mi gente, mi raza, together we can save
that one,
Let's speak up, a voice for all to keep a life from a gun.

My parents, they didn't say no, they showed me the
ability,
Our roots are deeper than division, it's of culture and
dignity.
Mi Gente, we too can make a difference in our
community,
It's up to us to give the next generation an
opportunity.

Rise up, speak up, together we can show love
Rise up, speak up, together we can show love

Mi gente, Mi Raza, Rise Up.

will leave no question in your mind of my truth:
I am grounded and I am a Mujer Grande!

By: Stephanie Salinas

I CAN'T BREATHE

I Can't Breathe

as a child I was blinded by the world of racism
into a teenager living it first hand in a new town one
nation

under God
indivisible
with liberty and justice for all
but I learned their all is systemically set up for
Black and Brown to fall

with racism
colorism
and discrimination
we will break these chains to be set free for a just
nation

spread out into the world united as one
George Floyd
Breonna Taylor
Sandy Guardiola
Anthony Baez
too many more
the time has come

to say Black Lives Matter loud and there's many levels
take it to Puerto Rico and look at our ghettos

unemployment at an all-time high
$7.25 pay
think the government wonders why?

poverty levels keep on topping
while the elite move in tax evading Brockin

law 22
law 60
opportunity Zone
crypto colonizers
jones act

By: Adassa

and wait there's more

opportunity after opportunity for our land and culture to be
repackaged and raped
minor investing in Boricuas to stay so they don't migrate to
escape

whitewashing the island
our saviors are here for gentrification on the make
protesting because for this we can no longer take

I can't breathe
living in systemic racism

I can't breathe
living in divided colorism

I can't breathe
with lack of medical care

I can't breathe
living under fragile infrastructure how can we bare

I can't breathe
with mass school closures and a poor educational system

I can't breathe
in an economic depression to push Boricuas out
Is that their mission?

I can't breathe
mismanagement and disparity to create a blank slate

I can't breathe
until the debt is cancelled Judge Swain it's not too late

We will breathe united to demand change
We will breathe for what needs to be dismantled and rearranged.

SINGING TO THE MOON

By: Mikayla Amina Brown

I sung to the moon
a song she knew
all too well

I sung the song
of my mother
of my grandmother
of my great-grandmother
of my ancestors

I sung of a day
where our children's worth
was not pre-determined
by a society that measures
us
based on the color of our
skin

I sung of a day
where our children's dreams
are not limited
by systematic measures
put in place to suppress us

I sung of a day
where our children's beauty
is not measured by
beauty standards that cater
to that of their Eurocentric
peers

I sung of a day
where our children's
differences
were a basis for unity
and not a basis for
divide

I sung of a day
where discrimination
is an unfamiliar concept
that, thankfully, our
children
will never know

I sung of a day
where love supersedes
hate

I sung of love
I sung of love
I sung of love.

ON HOW YOU ARE

By: Gianfranco Fernández-Ruiz

On the last Thursday of November next
I'll be three decades the boy who sat
and stared at a glass pilsner pitcher full
with glass eyes—
looking through to November next, seeing
how Mami and Abuelo would be—
how I would be.

And though I do not know yet,
it is the last Thursday
of Abuelo's Novembers.
In December he doesn't say goodbye.
His lungs fill up like the pilsner.
I'll be three times the boy he raised,
not yet my own. I wonder
how many times before this
have I been mami
or her abuelo? How many times
have drops of Presidente from that pilsner glass
dropped into my cup, where truth was,
into me, where they rippled
and rippled forever backward until
we were before God?

Or do the drops roll forward like dew
carried by the breeze
in a field of sugar cane before harvest,
vapor condensing? Does it fall from the sky,

into the ground, abuelo? Does it rise
from your grave to the aurora
until again I am before God,
having lived?

I was; I am
the pupil, a vessel, looking
at a reflection of a boy, upturned
decades earlier, a doll awash—
rippling, rippling, rippling.

Decades later, I with my children,
grandchildren.
I see mami in them—abuelo,
many other men and women I do not know
Is this the breeze
on the last Thursday of my Novembers.
They pour water for me at the dinner
table from the clear pilsner glass
I looked through.
I look through to them:
in the black of their pupils—the irises of God—
not yet their own, not yet distilled.

—my glass runneth over.

A STALK OF CANE WITH MY GRANDFATHER

By: Gianfranco Fernández-Ruiz

I gnawed a medium sized cane stalk
to pass the time.
My grandfather used to cut cane
and knew how to find good stalk—
"a faded green, almost yellow"
"thin and heavy" with "flesh off-white,
hard enough to tire the jaw;
it's to pass time after all", you'd be amazed
what things pass when chewing good
cane. When my wife told me that she was pregnant,
learned the baby would be a boy, I got cane
to pass the time.
—The secret is, my grandfather told me,
chew the moisture out—absorb the juices.
And if you swallow, time won't pass;
then you spit it out, leave it on a napkin
(that you're to carry
handily in your back pocket,
like a gentleman). And at some angles
it looks like the flayed
fibers of served pineapple,
at others, it looks like stacked toothpicks.
Luz, my son would tell me that he takes
the remains and makes houses with them,
he did that with dominoes too.
Another pasatiempo.
Can you believe that? Houses.
His grandmother remarks
"he will be an architect!"
That would be something else—
My grandchildren—architects.
I remember my grandfather
He would have laughed in vanity.

Even when the cancer
grew
from
his
leg
to
his
brain
he would have laughed—his great, great
grandchildren:
arquitectos.
"Great things do come with cane stalk."
I tell my great, great grandchildren:
"I ate some once, long ago,
and my grandfather came to me in a vision.
He promised I would have a boy in his stead,
and soon after, a daughter
who'd birth the white hairs on my head."
If I chewed a little longer,
he might have mentioned:
—the heart of the squash is only known
by the knife
—when there's no bread, cassava
—always please god and the devil
—curarse en salud
In my old age, I walk with a cane;
his cane. And the juices couldn't cure
the cancer in my leg; his cancer.
Only God knows, he used to say, and sugar cane,
is God's toothpick.
When I got the cancer of my grandfather,
I rarely chewed on cane,
or came around others who took part
in the pasatiempo. The few times I did
I chewed
and swallowed.

CPSIA information can be obtained
at www.ICGtesting.com
Printed in the USA
BVHW090525021220
594419BV00008BA/154

9 781734 725247